THE Endangered Florida Panther

THE Endangered Florida Panther

MARGARET GOFF CLARK

ILLUSTRATED WITH PHOTOGRAPHS

COBBLEHILL BOOKS
Dutton   New York

To my husband, CHAS. R. CLARK
If he weren't so helpful,
this book would not yet
be finished

Frontispiece: Florida panther in tree

The chapter entitled "Surprise Encounter" is an adaptation of an experience told to the author by David S. Maehr and also published in *Defenders* magazine (Sept/Oct 90). It is included with the permission of David Maehr and James Deane, editor of *Defenders*.

PHOTOGRAPH CREDITS: Chas. R. Clark, 48; Florida Game and Fresh Water Fish Commission, 6, 9; Melissa Foster, 32, 33; Dennis Jordan, 23; Kelly R. Pace, 44, 45; © 1991 Smithsonian Institution, Photo No. 77-7431, 12. All other photographs are by David S. Maehr. Map by Joseph Jakl.

Library of Congress Cataloging-in-Publication Data
Clark, Margaret Goff.
   The endangered Florida panther / Margaret Goff Clark.
      p.   cm.   Includes index.
   Summary: Examines the physical characteristics, habits, and natural environment of the endangered Florida panther and what is being done to save it from extinction.
   ISBN 0-525-65114-4
   1. Pumas—Florida—Juvenile literature.
2. Endangered species—Florida—Juvenile literature. [1. Pumas—Florida.
2. Rare animals.   3. Wildlife conservation.]   I. Title.
QL737.C23C53   1993   599.74'428—dc20   92-14816   CIP   AC

Published in the United States by Cobblehill Books,
an affiliate of Dutton Children's Books,
a division of Penguin Books USA Inc.,
375 Hudson Street, New York, New York 10014

Designed by Mina Greenstein   Printed in Hong Kong
First Edition   10 9 8 7 6 5 4 3 2 1

Acknowledgments

IN WRITING THIS BOOK about the Florida panther, I had help from many people.

David Maehr, Wildlife Biologist with the Florida Game and Fresh Water Fish Commission, shared with me his knowledge of the Florida panther, including many incidents from his years of working with this shy and endangered animal. He wrote the Introduction and supplied color photographs. In spite of his busy schedule, he tirelessly answered questions and checked the manuscript.

Dennis Jordan, Florida Panther Coordinator for the U.S. Fish & Wildlife Service, checked the manuscript and contributed color photographs for use in the book, as well as reports and studies of the panther and its problems.

Melissa Foster supplied unposed photos of animals traveling through the I-75 underpasses. Bill Burgin, Audio-Visual Specialist for the Game and Fresh Water Fish Commission, provided color photos of panthers.

The following members of the Florida Game and Fresh Water

Fish Commission provided information about the panther: Tom H. Logan, Chief, Bureau of Wildlife Research; Robert C. Belden and Jayde Roof, both wildlife biologists.

Peter Gallagher, President of Save the Florida Panther, Inc., and Dean M. Heflin, retired Professional Engineer at the Department of Transportation, also supplied information.

Claire Mackay and Isabel Hobba, friends and fellow writers, checked the manuscript in its early stages.

Noel and Bert MacCarry and Lila Church furnished voluntary panther news clipping services.

Contents

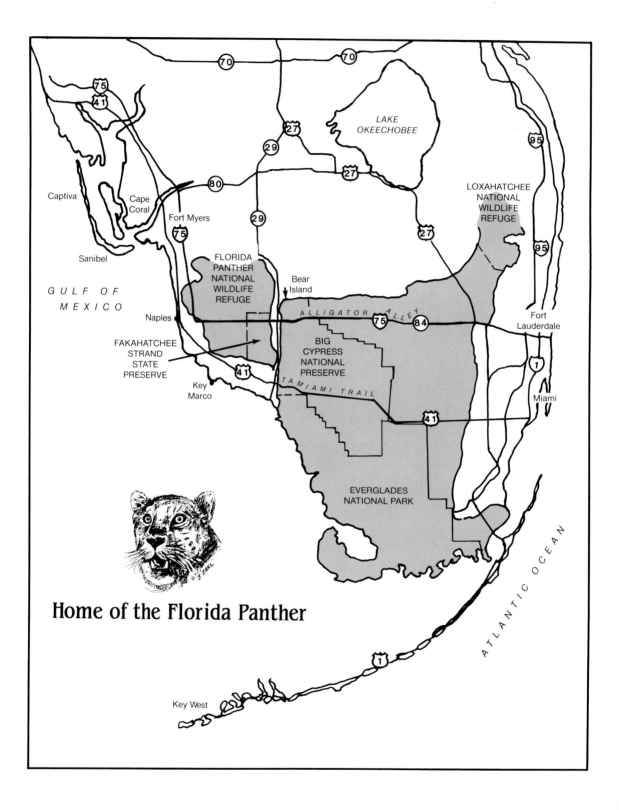

Home of the Florida Panther

Introduction

EVEN TO THOSE OF US who know the animal best, the Florida panther remains elusive and secretive. More than a decade of intense field research has answered many of the questions about its natural history and distribution. This information has been vital to a number of agencies as they take actions on behalf of the panther. The many successes resulting from this work are in large part a product of public interest in, and concern for, this large mysterious cat. But what does the future hold for the panther? More work and even greater successes will be necessary to insure that the panther remains a part of Florida's wild landscape.

The support of future generations of panthers can be encouraged with interesting accounts of the panther's day-to-day life and the problems it faces. Understanding the importance of big predators in maintaining a healthy environment for people is a lesson needed by everyone living in a world with less and less wildness. *The Endangered Florida Panther* will help harness the interest and imaginations of our children, and perhaps will be an investment in their future. Education is the first step in the process of appreciating and protecting our natural resources. Hopefully, this book will be that first step for many of our future decision-makers.

DAVID S. MAEHR
Wildlife Biologist
Florida Game and
Fresh Water Fish Commission

THE Endangered Florida Panther

1

How the Panther Lives

AT ONE TIME, the Florida panther lived throughout the southeastern United States. It ranged from Texas to the Atlantic coast and north into Tennessee. Today, only a few of these big cats remain. The Florida panther is one of the most endangered species.

Because this animal is shy and careful to keep out of sight of humans, its life has long been a mystery. Only recently has the dedicated work of naturalists made it possible for us to know how the Florida panther lives.

BEFORE HER kittens are born, the mother panther prepares a den for them. She looks for a dry place that is sheltered, so that animals or passing people will not know she and the babies are there.

Since the panther lives in southern Florida, the den does not have to be made warm. Often the mother chooses the middle of a saw palmetto thicket. There she clears an oval space large enough for her to lie down, then scrapes the dirt floor until it is smooth. The lacy fan-shaped palmetto leaves arch over the top of the den, hiding the creatures inside and giving some protection from sun and rain.

When it is time for the kittens to be born, the mother goes to the den. She may give birth to from one to four babies, each weighing about a pound. Although at first they cannot see, with a little help from their mother, they seem to have no trouble finding their way to her side to nurse. David Maehr, a biologist and panther researcher with the Florida Game and Fresh Water Fish Commission, described newborn kittens as "hairless little masses of muscle."

Opposite: A mother panther may choose a saw palmetto thicket for a den.
Below: A panther den seen from the inside

A panther kitten

The mother is the only one who cares for her kittens. Male panthers live alone, except when mating. In order to get food, the mother panther has to leave the kittens for as much as 36 hours at a time and may have to travel as far away as five miles. As soon as she is able to make a kill she eats as much as she can, then goes back to the den to nurse the kittens. The food that she eats helps to provide milk.

David Maehr explains, "The young apparently are able to fast for up to two days while the female is gone, and that's a remarkable feat for a small creature that has to maintain its body temperature and keep enough energy to survive."

Although the young can get along by themselves for a short time, the first six months of their lives are full of danger. If they stray from the den, they may get lost or carried away by an animal or bird of prey such as a hawk.

Studies have shown that panther kittens are better off when raised in a fertile area where there is vegetation for cover and food for large prey animals such as deer and wild hogs. The kittens' mother does not have to wear herself out traveling miles to find food, so she has more milk for her offspring and more hours to stay with them. The kittens are healthier and better able to survive than those reared on poor land with only small prey animals.

When the kittens are two to three weeks old, the mother increases her hunting time. This is because the kittens need more milk and they are old enough to stay alone longer. They now have wide-open blue eyes and their bodies are covered with light beige hair sprinkled with dark brown or blackish spots. On their tails are five rings the same color as the spots. At three weeks the kittens are the size of full-grown house cats.

While their mother is gone, the kittens play together. Apparently they also exercise their teeth and claws, for wildlife biologists who visited dens where kittens were raised found many stems of palmettos, greenbriar, and grapevine that were chewed and clawed.

For about two months the mother nurses her young. When they are six weeks of age, they can eat the meat their mother brings them.

As soon as the kittens are old enough, they travel with their mother all over her range of about 70 square miles, learning to hunt and to take care of themselves. Again and again they practice her way of creeping up on prey until they are close to it and can make a short, high-speed run for a quick attack. This method works well for panthers, for they are better sprinters than long-distance runners.

Most of the panthers' hunting is done at night, because that is when the prey animals they hunt are most likely to be roaming around. During the day the panthers rest in newly made day beds or in the den, if it is nearby.

As they grow, the kittens' appearance changes. The spots on their bodies and the rings on their tails gradually fade. At six months the markings are almost invisible. At the same time the young cats' blue eyes are turning brown and to the light straw color of an adult.

By the time the kittens are about a year-and-a-half old, they usually know how to hunt for themselves, killing small animals such as raccoons, rabbits, armadillos, and rats, as well as the occasional deer and wild hog. The older they get, the better they are at killing large prey.

When the kittens are about two years old, the mother is ready to mate again. At this time she takes the kittens to a kill and leaves them there. She does not come back, but she has made sure the young cats will have something to eat until they can find their own food.

At first the young ones stay together, but before long they wander off alone to start their adult lives. Although not yet full-grown, they look like their parents, with reddish-brown hair on the back, tan on the sides, and pale gray underneath. They usually have the typical Florida panther whorl of hair, or cowlick, in the middle of their backs and a kink at the end of their long tails.

The first problem of the young male cat beginning life alone is to find food. As soon as his stomach is full, he then sets out to locate a range of his own, the larger the better, and one that includes several females. If possible, he goes to well-drained land—a hardwood forest with deep, rich soil, or pine flatwoods. These are usually places where white-tailed deer and wild hogs are plentiful.

He soon discovers that most of the fertile lands have been taken by people for agriculture or citrus groves. The few that are left are already claimed by panthers that have marked the limits of their ranges with small piles of dirt and leaves on which they have left their own scent by urinating or defecating on them. These piles are called *scrapes*. When the young cat enters one of these ranges, marked by scrapes, the owner, usually a full-grown adult male, chases him off or starts a fight.

Panthers, especially the males, live by a rule which those who study the animal call the land tenure system. According to the rule, an animal has rights to a piece of land if he has been there longest. No matter if he is big and mean or small and ugly, if he was there first, he has prior rights. A 120-pound panther could defend his territory against one that might weigh 160 pounds. He has the psychological advantage of being in his home.

After days, or even months, of travel the young panther, if he's lucky, finds a range of mixed swamp and dry land whose owner has died. He marks the boundary with his own scent and soon makes a

An adult panther in the forest

day bed, similar to the den his mother prepared for her kittens. This is where he will spend the hottest hours of the day. At night he will go out to hunt. His eyes are fashioned to see well in the dark and to catch sight of even a slight motion. He will build a new day bed almost every day.

When he is full-grown he will be about seven feet long, from his nose to the tip of his tail, and will weigh from 100 to 160 pounds. At night he will go hunting inside his own range of 150 to 300 square miles. Daylight will find him in his day bed, resting.

The female panther is smaller than the male. She weighs from 65 to 100 pounds and is about six feet long from her nose to the tip of her tail.

Like her brother, she must find land of her own, but in some ways it is not quite as difficult for her. Apparently males do not see her as a threat. Often she is allowed to share a range with a male or another female. She needs a range where prey animals are plentiful, and a smaller amount of land is preferable so she does not have miles to travel for food for her kittens. Researchers have found that the average home area for the female panther is between 68 and 74 square miles.

Her life is not as lonely as her brother's, for by the time she is two to three years old, she will probably have kittens to keep her company much of the time.

Many people believe there are black panthers, but if a large black cat is seen, it is probably a leopard, escaped from a zoo, since true leopards come from Asia or Africa and are not native to the United States.

Ordinarily leopards are yellow or light brown with dark spots. Sometimes, though, they have a condition called *melanism* in which their hair is black. In any litter of leopard kittens, some may be born black. However, the true panther is never black.

2

Panther History

THERE IS PROOF that panthers lived in Florida as early as 500 to 600 years ago. One piece of evidence was discovered in 1896 by archaeologists digging on the tiny island of Key Marco off the southwestern coast of Florida.

Frank Hamilton Cushing, an archaeologist who was head of a group called the Pepper-Hearst Expedition, had been to Key Marco before and was eager to start finding the treasures he was sure were there.

Cushing and his assistants stood in water-filled trenches in a swamp where mangrove trees put down long snakelike roots into the water. Mosquitoes buzzed around the workers and the hot tropical sun beat down on their heads. Here, digging in black, smelly muck, the men uncovered beautiful masks and carvings fashioned many years ago by the Calusa Indians who had once lived on Key Marco. Although the works of art dug up by the archaeologists were made of wood, they were still in good condition.

One of the greatest treasures was a six-inch statue of a panther man or panther god that was carved of especially hard wood. The body of the kneeling figure resembled a person, but the head was that of a panther with huge round eyes and upright ears.

Later carbon tests made of material found at the same level as this little statue proved it dated from A.D. 1400–1500. The Key Marco Cat, as it is called, is now in the Smithsonian Institution in Washington, D.C.

The Key Marco cat,
A.D. *1400–1500*

Probably the panther lived in Florida even before the Key Marco Cat was carved. The cougar family, to which the Florida panther belongs, reaches far back into history. Before Europeans arrived here, the cougar lived throughout North and South America. This sturdy animal survived in every climate. According to the *Encyclopedia Americana*, "It was equally at home in subarctic snow and equatorial heat, in rain forest and desert, on mountain and plain."

When the white man arrived, taking over the wild lands and hunting with his gun, not even the tough cougar could stand up against him. Its numbers became fewer and fewer. Some still live in the western United States and in Canada, called by many different names—cougar, puma, panther, mountain lion, or catamount.

East of the Mississippi River the only known population of this once plentiful animal is in southern Florida. There it is called a panther.

The Florida panther (*Felis concolor coryi*) is a subspecies of the western cougar. For years it ranged over most of the southern United States east of the Mississippi River. Gradually the growth of population and the spread of agriculture pushed the panther into southern Florida. Separated by distance from the other species of cougar, it developed its own traits. It became smaller than the western cougar, with longer legs and smaller feet, but larger than Central American and Equatorial cougars. It is different from all the others in having an upward turn at the end of its long tail and a swirl of hair, a cowlick, on its back.

Like its relative, the western cougar, the Florida panther has had a hard time. To the Calusa Indians the panther may have been a god, but to the Europeans who came to settle in Florida it was a nuisance. They claimed it killed their livestock, and although there is no record of a panther attacking a human in Florida, the settlers were afraid of it.

The fears of the settlers led to laws being passed against panthers.

In 1832, when Florida was still a territory, the territorial legislature passed a law that paid people for killing panthers. In 1887, after Florida became a state, another law approved a five-dollar bounty for every panther scalp turned in.

One of the many hunters was a young man named Charles Barney Cory. He must have had a special interest in nature, because he was Curator of Ornithology (the study of birds) in the Boston Society of Natural History, and was also a member of several organizations for the study of birds, plants, and animals. In his book, *Hunting and Fishing in Florida,* published in 1896, Cory told about one of his days hunting the panther. This is what happened.

One morning in 1895, Charles Cory and members of his hunting group awakened early. The five men, five horses, and six trained hunting dogs were camped in a wilderness area about 35 miles south of Lantana, on the eastern side of Florida. One of the men, John Davis, was a hunting guide. After a light breakfast, the men mounted their horses and, with their dogs running before them, rode into the dense woods for a day of panther hunting. Cory was eager to take a photograph of a panther.

During the day the hunters separated. Davis, the guide, and one of the other men, led by some of the dogs, found a female panther. When she ran up a tree, Davis wounded her in the hind feet, hoping to keep her until Cory could take her picture. The panther, in spite of her injured feet, jumped from the tree and ran away, followed by the dogs.

Cory, hurrying in the direction of the barking hounds, discovered the injured panther hiding under a large fallen tree in a cypress swamp. He could not take a picture of her there and, instead, he shot her.

Following the sound of the gunfire, Davis and his companion joined Cory and carried the dead panther to a clearing at the edge of the swamp.

One of the men photographed Cory bending over the body of the

Cypress swamps are home to the Florida panther.

beautiful animal. Realizing that the panther he had killed was unusually fine, Cory measured her carefully and later described her in his book.

He said his panther was about seven feet from her nose to the tip of her tail, and that her feet were smaller and her legs longer than a Colorado panther of about the same length.

Cory was the first person to describe the Florida panther as a separate subspecies of panther. He called it *Felis concolor floridana*. *Felis concolor* means cat of one color, not striped like the tiger or spotted like the leopard. It turned out that the name *floridana* had already been added to the scientific name for a Florida bobcat. After years of study by scientists, it was decided that the Florida panther should be named *Felis concolor coryi*, after the man who first described this subspecies.

As the years passed and more and more people moved into Florida, the panther was squeezed farther south into the Everglades and Big Cypress Swamp, to which people rarely came. But more thousands of settlers moved to Florida every year. They built homes, cities grew up. Parts of the wild lands where the panthers lived were cleared of trees and the ground was plowed for farms to feed the newcomers. Because of the frost-free climate, citrus groves and vegetable farms were planted. Even the swamplands where some panthers had taken refuge began to be drained.

Gradually, farmers realized that the panther was not as much a danger to their livestock as they had thought. The animal was shy, and stayed away from people.

In 1950, Florida declared the panther was a game species and could be hunted only during the open deer season.

In 1958, it was removed from the game list and given complete protection.

The national government passed the Endangered Species Act of 1973, which included the Florida panther.

In 1976, the U.S. Fish & Wildlife Service appointed the Panther Recovery Team, which prepared the Florida Panther Recovery Plan, deciding on steps that needed to be taken to save the panther.

Biologist Chris Belden and associates began the Florida Game and Fresh Water Fish Commission's search for populations of panthers.

In 1978, the Florida Panther Act made the killing of a panther a felony, a serious crime.

Agencies such as the Florida Panther Technical Advisory Council and the Florida Panther Interagency Committee were formed to study the needs of the panther and to search for ways to save it.

In 1982, the Florida panther was given a great honor. It was named the Florida state animal. This was a turning point, making citizens of Florida aware of the national treasure that was in danger of being lost. Panthers turned up in newspapers and on television. Public support grew.

Still, in spite of the honor placed on its handsome head, the laws to protect it, and the work of the agencies, no more than fifty Florida panthers are left, according to estimates of naturalists who work with panthers. And some of the remaining big cats are not healthy. How much longer can they last?

3

Collaring a Panther

FOR YEARS the panther has roamed through the wilderness in southern Florida, but few people have ever seen it. They might find fresh paw prints and notice a swaying of the long grass, but that would be all.

In October, 1976, biologist Chris Belden started the Florida Game and Fresh Water Fish Commission's panther search. When he and the other members of the Commission began, they didn't know if a living, reproducing group of panthers still existed in Florida. They looked for panther signs, such as paw prints, scrapes, and kills, and set up a central filing system to record all reports of panthers. To their delight they found three populations of panthers, all in the Big Cypress and Everglades sections of Florida.

It was not until 1981, when they added the tools of modern science to their own mental and physical work, that they began to solve the mystery. Since then the wildlife researchers have collected a great deal of information. They know how much land and what kind of land panthers need, what they eat, what their health problems are, and how they live day by day. They learned of this and more by radio-collaring the panthers.

Putting a collar on a live panther is not easy.

The researchers set out before daybreak dressed in sturdy clothes and sometimes with high, waterproof footgear.

"Most of the time we wear low sneakers," says biologist David Maehr. "They dry fast, and we don't see many snakes."

Usually at least four people work together on this project, one of them a veterinarian. They take a truck as close as possible to the area where the panthers live, then continue on foot. Each person has to carry a heavy load of equipment.

With them is a houndsman, usually R.T. McBride, and his three well-trained "cat" dogs, described by Maehr as "our most talented furred and four-legged friends."

The dogs lead the way, sniffing for the scent of a panther. When they get onto the trail of one, they race after it, barking excitedly. Sometimes the panther escapes, but usually the dogs are able to follow it. When the pack draws near, the panther climbs a tree. The dogs keep up their guard, yipping and standing on their hind legs, pawing at the tree trunk.

When the team members reach the tree, they begin work on the problem of getting the panther down and captured without injury to it. With only 30 to 50 panthers still left in Florida, every one is important.

Knowing that some treed mountain lions in the western part of the United States have died in falls, the Florida biologists use a portable, inflatable cushion to prevent such tragedies.

They quickly spread out a large, round, nylon cloth with seven pockets evenly spaced around the circle. The workers blow up plastic trash bags, tie them with twine, and stuff them into the pockets. When filled, the cushion contains about thirty trash bags. The biologists, now somewhat out of breath, place the air-filled cushion on the ground below the treed panther. Above this cushion they hold a nylon rope net.

Above: Jayde Roof climbing tree to lower panther to the ground

Left: A panther hound is trained to pick up the scent of a panther.

One member of the team, a specialist in anesthetics, studies the panther to estimate its general condition. He then shoots it in the thigh with a measured dose of medication. It is important to use the right kind of drug and the appropriate amount for the animal, just enough to put it to sleep for a short time.

If the panther is resting safely in the tree, a team member, usually biologist Jayde Roof, climbs up, ties a rope around the sleeping animal, and lowers it to the net.

In case the panther accidentally falls out of the tree, it drops onto the net with the cushion under it and is assured of a soft landing.

Working swiftly while the cat is still asleep, the veterinarian and the biologists check to see if it is ill or injured. If it has simple problems, the team cares for them at once. On the rare occasion when additional medical attention is needed, they send the panther to a zoo where it can receive the care it needs.

When the captured panther has no illness or injuries, the veterinarian and biologists, working together, weigh it, draw blood, and take other biological samples for testing later. They also check its teeth, and give the animal shots for protection from diseases common to panthers, such as rabies and feline leukemia.

The researchers then fasten a radio collar around its neck, adjusting it carefully for comfort and safety. The collar is about two inches wide and weighs a pound and a half. Its signal can be heard on land for a mile and a half and for 15 miles in the air. Each collar has its own signal.

The researchers often keep track of as many as twenty collared panthers roaming over approximately two million acres. Three times a week they go up in an airplane outfitted with special antennas which pick up signals from the collars. These signals tell whether the panther is resting or moving around and make it possible for the biologists to find the animal. They then record its location on a map. Back at the office they put the information into a computer. With its help they

Panther in nylon rope net with air-filled cushion below

make maps that show where the panther is traveling, what other panthers it is meeting, and how often it crosses roads. These facts are important in learning if a panther has enough land on which to live, how far it has to travel to obtain food, and even when a female has given birth to kittens.

The transmitter on the collar reports on the panther's condition. The beat is caused by the animal's movement, not by its pulse. An

Biologists and veterinarian work together to examine a panther and attach a radio collar.

irregular beat from the collar indictates the animal is moving. If the panther does not move in at least two hours, the transmitter is programmed to turn on a fast beat, announcing that the panther probably is not alive. When the biologists locate the dead animal, they perform an autopsy to find out what caused its death.

The lack of a beat may be because the transmitter is not working properly. The battery usually lasts for two years and then must be replaced.

When the team members finish collaring the panther, they remove the animal from the net and step aside, waiting until the cat wakes up and walks or runs away. They know it is wiser to stand behind a wide-awake panther than in front of it.

In an interview, David Maehr said, "I have heard critics through the years questioning what collars do to affect behavior of the animals. We think it doesn't interfere at all, and may in fact be important in helping us to protect them.

"We had a young female panther on routine recapture. Her old collar was about to go out. We noticed one rear foot was maimed and mangled. She had been shot in the foot. There were pieces of lead, broken bones. While we had her on the ground we saw the foot was about an inch shorter than the other rear foot. The healing process had begun, but there was *necrotic* [dead] bone sticking out through the skin.

"We were concerned about infection, systemic infection that eventually would kill her. So we kept her in captivity for about a month. We cleaned out the wound, removed the necrotic bone, and put her back in the wild about a month later. Today she is raising two kittens in the Fakahatchee Strand. We feel we've done her a service and the panther population as well, to have another female in the wild, able to have more kittens."

The work of the panther researcher can be rewarding, amusing, dangerous, or all three.

4

Surprise Encounter

DAVID MAEHR strode through the south Florida woodland, waving his arms now and then to chase off the mosquitoes that buzzed around his head.

It was late morning on a hot August day, and Maehr was checking out an area where the big cats lived. His work was to learn as much as possible about the few panthers that were still alive, with the hope of helping to save them from disappearing forever.

As always, Maehr was alert for such signs of panther as paw prints or bones of deer or wild hog that might be the remains of a big cat's dinner. From years of experience in his work, Maehr knew the Florida panther almost always disappeared before a human came near.

Suddenly he jolted to an abrupt stop. About fifty feet ahead he saw a full-grown panther stretched out at the foot of a tree. At once Maehr knew it was a female because four sleeping spotted kittens were with her. The mother panther is the parent that cares for the offspring, usually until they are one-and-a-half years old. He also recognized her as Female Number 19 by the collar she wore that identified her with a special radio signal.

Too often he and the other researchers had looked for panthers for days without a glimpse of one. And here was a scene from the daily life of these hard-to-find creatures.

He could not resist walking toward the five cats, noticing how the dark reddish-brown fur on the mother's back blended with the tree trunks, while the green palmetto fronds formed a colorful backdrop.

Maehr could scarcely believe his good luck. Now he was close enough to see the mother's stiff white whiskers.

One of the kittens sat up and stared directly at Maehr with babyish brown eyes. Maehr paused and held his breath, afraid it would set up a warning cry. But the kitten only yawned, showing sharp white teeth, then lay down beside the mother's front feet. The big cat raised her head and swatted at an insect, but she, too, went back to resting.

David Maehr is always alert to panther signs like this male track in the mud.

To Maehr's dismay, a twig snapped some distance back in the woods. He knew it must be his field partner, Jayde Roof, coming to join him.

The mother sat up and looked in the direction of the sound.

Maehr was now only twenty feet from the cats. Realizing he couldn't get away without being noticed, he froze. Even if he could escape, he still did not want to leave and miss seeing how a panther would behave in this situation.

As the roving eyes of the big cat found Maehr, she let out a deep growl. This sent the kittens hurrying behind her and across an open space of dried mud, tumbling over each other in their haste. Within seconds they had disappeared into a clump of palmetto.

Their mother turned her head as if to be sure they were safe, then began to walk toward the intruder at a slow but determined pace. Maehr knew she was stalking him.

He took a step backward, then another. And another. The cat's alert eyes stayed on his, and when he took a step, so did she.

In all the times Maehr and his associates had come close to a panther while studying its way of life, the cat had always sensed they were near and walked away before they arrived. He began to regret his curiosity.

While nervously matching steps with Number 19, he could imagine how a deer might feel when it was about to be dinner for a panther.

He knew there had never been a report of a panther attacking a human in Florida. Now he wondered if he were about to be first. After all, she had kittens to protect. That might make an alarming difference.

With his eyes still meeting the panther's, he continued to back up, taking longer and longer steps, gradually increasing the distance between them.

He saw that the panther's gaze was beginning to wander and she was walking more slowly. Now that there was more space between them, perhaps she no longer feared he was a danger to her kittens.

Maehr turned and walked away, trying not to hurry. When he glanced back, he saw that Number 19 was not following him. Before long he met Jayde Roof, who had been silently observing the encounter.

"I'm surprised," said Jayde. "She stood watching you before she went away. That's strange. You know panthers always leave first."

Maehr wiped perspiration from his forehead. "Someone should tell that to Number 19."

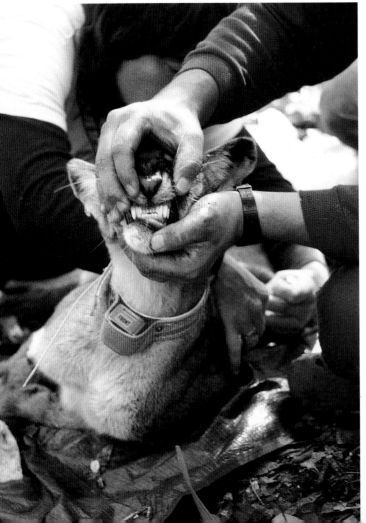

Left: Female Number 19 had been captured earlier and a radio collar attached.

Opposite: Jayde Roof, seen here with a male panther, was Maehr's field partner when he encountered Female Number 19.

5

Alligator Alley

IN THE EARLY 1960s, when plans were made for building State Road 84 across Florida, arguments such as this were heard:

"There'll be a lot of accidents on a narrow two-lane road." "It will cost too much to build. Imagine cutting a road across the Everglades where there are all those swamps and trees." "And alligators! They ought to call it Alligator Alley."

The name, Alligator Alley, caught on. Soon that was what almost everyone began to call State Road 84. The road was built and used for many years. But as time went on, and traffic increased, too many people were being killed on the busy, narrow road.

The Florida panther was also a victim. Alligator Alley passed through Fakahatchee Strand State Preserve, the Everglades, and Big Cypress National Preserve, all of them home to the panther and other endangered species.

From 1979 to November, 1989, twelve panthers were killed by cars or trucks on southwest Florida roads, five of them on Alligator Alley. Dusk and night were especially hazardous times. Most of the panther's travel is after dark. Too often a driver could not see the less than three-foot-high panther running across the road until it was too late. The result was often tragedy for both human and animal.

Hoping to improve across-the-state travel, the Florida Department of Transportation (DOT) planned to widen Alligator Alley and make it part of the interstate system. Its new name would be I-75.

Officials said that a four-lane highway would save many people because vehicles would not bump into each other trying to pass, as they did on the narrow road. Also, the speed limit would be raised to the 65 miles-per-hour limit, common on Florida's four-lane highways. This would cut down travel time between Naples on the west coast and Fort Lauderdale on the east.

Those interested in saving the panther said, "That's fine for humans, but it doesn't help the panther. The big cats will just have to run farther and faster to cross the road."

The Florida Game and Fresh Water Fish Commission and the U.S. Fish & Wildlife Service tackled the program. They considered putting up 45 miles-per-hour signs in areas where panthers crossed, but they decided that speed limit would be too difficult to enforce. Keeping the panthers off the road would also be impossible. Since the road cut through their homeland, they naturally would continue to cross for food and mating.

The solution was to build wildlife underpasses at intervals along the 76-mile road. The work could be done while Alligator Alley, now to be I-75, was being widened.

Tom Logan, Bureau Chief of Wildlife Research for the Florida Game and Fresh Water Fish Commission, and Gary Evink, Chief Ecologist for the Department of Transportation, were leaders in the design and location of the underpasses.

When it came to deciding where to place the underpasses, they went to computer studies that showed where radio-collared panthers often crossed. Records kept by the biologists also listed where panthers had been killed trying to cross.

The planners decided that thirty-six underpasses, each eight feet tall and 100 feet wide, would be built under the highway.

Above: I-75 underpass

Left: A deer in I-75 underpass

Below: Alligator going through underpass on former Alligator Alley

Opposite: Bobcat in underpass

How would panthers and other animals know they should use the underpasses? The planners had an answer to that. A tall fence would be built on either side of the new road, so that animals would cross only at the places built for them.

When several of the underpasses were finished, remote-control sensing cameras were installed by University of Florida researcher Melissa Foster to find out if animals were using their special crossings. According to an Associated Press article in the April 21, 1990, Fort Myers *News-Press*, the first roll of film developed showed "a radio-collared panther, four deer, and a man on a motorcycle. The only one who didn't belong there was the man. It was illegal for him to be in the panther refuge area or the underpass."

Don Wood, Endangered Species Coordinator for the Game and Fish Commission, told the Tampa *Tribune*, "Nobody knew if those things [the underpasses] would work, and lo and behold, they do. We have to assume if one [panther] will use them, other panthers will, too."

Later rolls of film showed bobcats, opossums, raccoons, an alligator, and another panther also taking advantage of the safe undercrossings.

A toll of one dollar to be charged at each end of the road was planned to cover the expense of constructing the wildlife crossings. The tolls would stop when the total cost of approximately 14 million dollars was collected.

6

Mystery of
Cat Number 12

CAT NUMBER 12 was a fine, healthy 122-pound panther, one of the first male cats to be collared. He was captured on January 2, 1986, in Bear Island, an area of southwestern Florida north of Big Cypress National Preserve.

Ever since his collar had been put in place, the biologists had been able to keep track of him. They knew where his spacious 300-square-mile range was and how far he traveled in search of food. They even learned what other panthers, male and female, he was seeing.

As time went on, he fathered at least five litters of kittens, perhaps seven. He seemed to be the outstanding male resident of his area. Many times he had crossed the old Alligator Alley, now I-75. The biologists realized it took a wise and careful cat to make that crossing without getting run over. As David Maehr, research biologist, re-marked, "He seemed to combine all the qualities of a successful panther, intelligence and a fair amount of luck."

In November, 1988, the signal from Number 12's collar became slower and slower. On December 13 there was no signal at all. From then on there was only silence from Cat Number 12. The worried biologists tried to track him on the ground, but they could not find him. The lack of a signal from the collar did not indicate the panther was dead, but it did mean there was something wrong with the transmitter. Without it, the biologists could not keep in touch with the big cat with which they had been in contact for almost two years.

Early in January, 1989, a construction worker who was helping to build underpasses on the improved Alligator Alley, phoned the office of the Florida Game and Fish Commission.

"We've found a dead panther in an underpass," he said.

At once biologists from the Commission hurried to Alligator Alley, afraid of what they would find. To their relief, the dead animal was a bobcat.

"We were disappointed to lose a bobcat," said David Maehr, "but we were relieved that it was not our old friend, Panther Number 12."

On the weekend of January 14 and 15, Maehr and other team members took time off from their search for the missing cat.

On the 15th, the houndsman Roy McBride went out with his dogs, as he did every day to keep up their strength and their knowledge of what they were supposed to do. Suddenly, the dogs came across a panther and chased it up a tree. It was Number 12.

At once McBride began to round up all the people who were necessary to catch a panther. David Maehr was the hardest to find because he was in Sarasota. That was only two hours away, but it took time for his coworkers to contact him.

When Maehr finally reached the panther refuge with refuge manager Todd Logan, they climbed into the swamp buggy that had been left behind for them and started toward the scene of action. However, in a few minutes they became stuck in a large mud hole. As soon as they managed to maneuver out of it, they found themselves trapped even deeper in another hole. That time they had to winch the swamp buggy out.

Cat Number 12 waiting in tree

They were the last to reach the tree where the big cat was still sitting. All the other workers were there and had the cushion and nylon net in place. It was 5:30 in the afternoon. Since it was winter, the sun would soon go down. By the time they had the panther on the ground, it was dark.

With the help of lights from the swamp buggy, they examined Cat Number 12. Maehr remarked, "He looks as if he's been through a meat grinder."

The panther's ears were torn and he had scars all over his body, plus a skin rash. His left foot had been broken or dislocated, but now was healing. There seemed to be nothing seriously wrong with him. The biologists cleaned him up and took care of his injuries.

When they removed his collar, they discovered a small hole in the radio transmitter. It was about the size of the end of a little finger.

Todd Logan helping to treat a panther

The hole was not round enough to have been made by a bullet and it did not go all the way through, as a bullet probably would have done. To the left of the hole they noticed a dent in the collar. This gave them the idea that an animal might have made the hole.

The biologists fitted Number 12 with a new collar and set him free.

Maehr took the old collar back to the office with him. On his bookshelf he had the skull of a mountain lion, very much like the skull of a panther. When Maehr placed the skull against Cat Number 12's old radio collar, one front tooth fitted into the hole that had penetrated the transmitter and another matched up with the dent in the collar.

When Maehr discussed this with the other biologists, they attacked the problem like detectives. Little by little they began to figure out what had happened. They agreed that Cat Number 12 had gotten into a fight with another panther. They believed his opponent was a male cat, Number 25. He was about the same size as Number 12, but he was younger, and maybe not as strong and experienced. Number 25 had died some time ago from an infection, perhaps caused by bacteria entering his body from the claws or teeth of Number 12. He had not been seriously injured, but the infection could have brought about his death.

During the fight between the two animals, Number 25 must have bitten Number 12's collar so hard his tooth had gone through the heavy-gauge brass that covered the radio transmitter. The transmitter had continued to work for two or three months, until enough moisture seeped in to short-circuit it.

Cat Number 12 is still running around on his 300-square-mile range, unaware that his life may have been saved by his radio collar.

7

Is There Hope?

MELODY ROELKE, veterinarian and panther researcher, was puzzled. It was 1986, and she was helping to care for the panthers in Everglades National Park. To her surprise, the panthers she examined did not have the usual kink at the end of their tails or the cowlick of hair on their backs. These were the trademarks of the real Florida panther. All the panthers in Big Cypress Swamp where she had worked before had had these signs. Did that mean the Everglades panthers were mixed breeds?

This could be a serious problem. Ever since the passage of the Endangered Species Act in 1973, the United States government had given money to pay for protecting all endangered species, for research to help them, and to preserve the wild lands where they lived. However, there was no federal assistance given if the species were hybrid, not purebred.

The genetic differences in the Florida panthers had long been known, but until this time, they had not become an issue.

As the word of Melody Roelke's news spread, the federal govern-

Panther in tree. The crook at end of its tail is proof that it is a real Florida panther.

ment asked her and another scientist, Stephen J. O'Brien, to find out the genetic facts about the Florida panthers.

The two scientists went to work in O'Brien's laboratory at the National Cancer Institute in Frederick, Maryland.

After three years of studying the genes of the panthers, Roelke and O'Brien suggested that the grandparents of a few Florida panthers might have mated with some South American cougars, possibly captives that were released by an Everglades tourist attraction between 1957 and 1967. Although this probably strengthened the panthers in Florida, it made some of them mixed breeds. This could mean that federal funds would no longer help to care for the endangered panther.

Panther habitat from the air. Oak and palmetto woods, the kind of land best for the Florida panther.

The management of the Endangered Species Act was in the hands of the U.S. Fish & Wildlife Service. They had the power to alter policies under the act. After several weeks of study, they decided that all wild panthers in Florida would be equally protected.

The United States government was still in the fight to save the Florida panther.

EVEN WITH government help, it is uncertain whether or not the Florida panther will keep on running through the woodlands. It is still one of the world's most endangered species. However, its chances are better than they were a few years ago, because its needs are no longer a mystery.

After years of study, researchers have learned that the key to saving the panther is land, but not just any land. It needs fertile, forested wilderness. Almost every problem the panther has is a land problem.

Because of its limited habitat, the panther population is small, making every individual important. Every death temporarily shrinks the already dangerously low numbers which lead to inbreeding.

If we do not want Florida's proud, wild, state animal to be reduced to a tame cat in a zoo, we need to give it space. If it has room, it can help to rebuild its own numbers.

The panther is a keystone species; that is, other creatures depend on it for support. The land we preserve for the panther also protects thousands of smaller animals and other creatures that run, crawl, or fly.

The panther's needs and ours are related. Saving the wilderness helps to protect Florida's limited water supply, promotes clean air, and contributes to preserving the ozone layer.

If we maintain the wild lands already set aside and add to them, that could be our best gift to the panther and our future generations.

The Florida panther is in trouble, but it is no longer alone. With the help of its many friends and its own strong spirit there is hope.

8

Captive Breeding

IT WAS DECEMBER, 1990. In some ways life was getting better for the Florida panthers.

They now had panther medical care. If they were sick or injured, a biologist or veterinarian came to take care of them.

Once or twice a year they were vaccinated for a number of diseases.

Besides, there were the underpasses. Panthers out for the night could travel to the far side of highway I-75 and back without getting hit by a car.

In spite of these improvements, the big cats were not increasing in numbers, and since there were so few left, they often were mating with relatives. This inbreeding was bad for the health of the kittens, and as the years go on, could lead to the end of the species.

This was why in December, 1990, the U.S. Fish & Wildlife Service approved a captive breeding plan. It seemed worth trying. Captive breeding had been successful with other endangered species, such as the red wolf and the black-footed ferret.

The biologists of the Florida Game and Fresh Water Fish Commission had kept track of the family records of all panthers they had collared. With the help of this information, they were ready to choose up to six kittens and four adults with as wide genetic backgrounds as possible, so that the chosen panthers would not have to mate with relatives.

These panthers would be taken to carefully selected zoos where it was hoped they would produce healthy kittens that, when they were grown and properly conditioned, could be released in the wild. The captive-born panthers could start colonies in different parts of the state, or elsewhere within the historic range of the panther.

Many questions were raised. Would taking adult cats from the

Veterinarian Melody Roelke with the first panther kitten captured for captive breeding program

Close-up of first panther kitten taken for captive breeding

population upset the balance of life on the panther ranges and perhaps cause fights? With this in mind, only kittens under a year old would now be taken.

The most difficult question of all was, where could land be found for the new cats when they were old enough to be on their own?

Not all problems could be solved ahead of time. It was decided to start the breeding program soon, while the few healthy panthers were alive and able to produce kittens. This was the winter season, the best time to remove the cats that were to be taken for breeding. In the cooler weather they would feel less stress.

An article in the February 21, 1991, Fort Myers *News-Press* announced that on Wednesday, February 20, the first panther kitten, a seven-month-old male, was caught after he was chased up a palm tree by hounds. He was described as being slightly smaller than a German shepherd dog.

Darrell Land, a state wildlife biologist who hauled equipment for the capture team, said, "He [the cat] weighed 34 pounds and appeared to be quite healthy. He still had some of his baby teeth, or kitten teeth, if you like to call them that."

On Wednesday, May 8, 1991, the *News-Press* announced:

PANTHER KITTEN GOAL MET

Goals for the 1991 phase of the state's captive breeding program have been met with the capture of six kittens. "Three males and three females have been removed from the wild," said Tom Logan, Bureau Chief for the Florida Game and Fresh Water Fish Commission.

The sixth kitten had been captured on May 6, 1991.

Adminstrators of the captive breeding program expect the offspring born of the kittens caught in 1991 will be returned to the wild in ten years.

By the year 2001 the land may be available for the captive-born panthers. Actions are underway to preserve as much of the remaining panther habitat as possible. But if land development in Florida continues to spread as it did from 1981 to 1991, wild land may be even scarcer when the panthers leave the zoos.

It doesn't have to be that way, though. We can begin now to set aside more wilderness land. The endangered Florida panther and other wild creatures of this world need room to live.

9

To See a Panther

I WANTED TO SEE a panther, a real Florida panther, living in the wilderness.

"You could look years and never see one," said one of the researchers who had helped me gather information for this book. "Look at all the trouble we go through to collar a panther. We spot them from the air, and track them down with dogs."

"So, I could go along."

"We're not allowed to take people with us. Too dangerous."

I sighed. "There must be some way I can see a panther."

"Sure. Go to a wildlife attraction. There are several around here."

"But will I see a panther?"

"Probably not," he admitted. "But you'll see cougars, and they look like Florida panthers except for the kink at the end of the tail and the cowlick on the back."

The first attraction I visited had acres of fenced land where animals could roam. There I saw a large reddish-brown animal stretched out beneath a tree.

Above: Lady, the purring cougar at Babcock Wilderness Adventures

Left: The author holding Shelly Star

Steve, the guide, made a kissing noise with his mouth and said quietly, "Come on, Lady."

The animal raised her head, with rounded ears upright, as if listening.

"She looks like a panther," I said. "Her tail has a kink."

"She may be a Florida panther, but we can't be sure she's pure-bred, so we call her a cougar. There isn't much difference."

Steve repeated the kissing sound, and Lady lazily and regally stood up.

Like a queen reviewing her troops, the cougar paced in front of her visitors, only three or four feet from us on the other side of a wire fence.

She looked up with expressive brown eyes, and when I talked to her as if she were a pet, I heard her deep, contented purr, like the amplified purr of a house cat. It made a shiver of excitement go up my back. Whatever she was, panther or cougar, she was a magnificent animal.

At the second wildlife attraction, I had an unusual opportunity. On the porch of one of the buildings was a child's playpen, screened on top and sides. Inside was a lively cougar kitten. One of the attendants lifted the kitten, named Shelly Star, and put her into my arms.

Although she was only three-and-a-half weeks old, she was the size of a full-grown domestic cat. Her eyes were kitten-blue and her pale gray fur was dotted with blackish spots. Rings of the same color circled her tail.

Shelly Star was playful and, like most kittens, wanted to chew on my fingers, but one look at her white, needle-sharp teeth convinced me that was not my game. When I petted her, she settled down on my lap and posed for her picture.

Lady and Shelly Star are tame cats, friendly because they always have lived with people who fed them and treated them kindly. They look like wild cougars or panthers, except that they do not have the wilderness in their eyes.

Places in Florida where you may see a panther or cougar:

Babcock Wilderness Adventures
Route 31
Punta Gorda, FL 33982
(813) 489-3911

Everglades Wonder Gardens
On old U.S. 41
Bonita Springs, FL 33923
(813) 992-2591

Octagon Wildlife Sanctuary
41660 Horseshoe Road
Punta Gorda, FL 33955
(813) 543-1130

Jungle Larry's Zoological Park at
Caribbean Gardens
1590 Goodlette Road
Naples, FL 33940
(813) 262-5409

Tallahassee Junior Museum
3945 Museum Drive
Tallahassee, FL 32310
(904) 575-8684

To help the Florida panther:

Send a tax-deductible donation to:
Florida Panther Research and
Management Trust Fund
Florida Game and Fresh Water
Fish Commission
620 South Meridian Street
Tallahassee, FL 32399-1600

Or join:
Save the Florida Panther, Inc.
P.O. Box 22369
Fort Lauderdale, FL 33335

Make check payable to:
Florida Game and Fresh Water
Fish Commission, with notation
that it is for the Trust Fund

Florida Panther Milestones

1832   When Florida was a territory, not yet a state, the territorial legislature passed a law to pay people for killing panthers.

1887   A Florida law set a $5.00 bounty for each panther scalp

1950   Florida declared the panther a game species to be hunted only
during open deer season

1958   The panther was removed from the game list and given complete
protection throughout Florida

1973   The U.S. Government passed the Endangered Species Act of
1973, which included the Florida panther

1976   Panther Recovery Team appointed by the U.S. Fish & Wildlife
Service (F&WS). The team prepared the Florida Panther Recovery
Plan

1976   Biologist Chris Belden and associates began the Florida Game and Fresh Water Fish Commission's search for populations of panthers

1978   The Florida Panther Act made the killing of a panther a felony, a serious crime

1981   The Game and Fish Commission began to radio-collar panthers and to study their needs

1982   The Florida panther was named the Florida state animal

1983   Florida State Legislature established the Florida Panther Technical Advisory Council

1986   The Florida Panther Interagency Committee was established, made up of representatives from U.S. Fish & Wildlife Service, Florida Game and Fresh Water Fish Commission, National Park Service, and Florida Department of Natural Resources

1987   Florida Panther Recovery Plan was revised and brought up-to-date

1991   Underpasses were built under I-75, so that panthers and other animals could cross in safety.

1991   Panther captive breeding began

Index